F-1 Reinstatement Petition

ATTORNEY BRIAN D. LERNER

Law Offices of Brian D. Lerner, A Professional Corporation

Attorney Brian D. Lerner

F-1 Reinstatement Petition

F-1 Reinstatement Petition

Written by Attorney Brian D. Lerner

Disclaimer and Terms of Use:

Effort has been made to ensure that the information in this book is accurate and complete. However, the author and the publisher do not warrant that this particular petition will mirror or be exactly as your situation. There has not been any attorney-client agreement created by the purchase of this petition or application. No legal advice has occurred. The cases, regulations and/or statutes cited may change at any time without notice.

Print ISBN: 978-1-948774-84-0
Ebook ISBN: 978-1-948774-83-3

INTRODUCTION

There are a multitude of different immigration petitions and applications. They are complex and full of requirements. Obviously it would be best to hire and immigration attorney to best prepare the petitions and application. However, this can certainly cost thousands of dollars.

The next best option is to get a sample of the petition written by an experienced immigration attorney. The samples cost a fraction what would be charged by an immigration attorney. However, while the reader has to alter, amend and change the parts of the sample petition to reflect their actual situation, it is a fantastic roadmap for them to use. If the reader has purchased the entire petition or application, they will have real live samples of cover letters, forms, declarations, affidavits and the necessary exhibits to use. The samples come from real cases and the names of those clients have been redacted to protect the privacy of that person or corporation.

These are petitions and applications that have been drafted by an experienced immigration attorney with over 25 years of experience. Get the benefits of that experience without the costs.

About the Law Offices of Brian D. Lerner

The Law Offices of Brian D. Lerner, APC. The law practice consists of Immigration and Nationality Law and everything involved with and regarding immigration which includes citizenship, investment visas, family and employment visas, removal and deportation hearings, appeals, waivers, adjustment, consulate processing and all types of immigration and citizenship matters. Thousands of families have been reunited and/or permitted to stay in the U.S. and/or return to the U.S. because of the successful work of Immigration Attorney Brian D. Lerner.

This law offices handles all types of immigration cases including family based and employment based. Immigration issues range from immigration court proceedings to trying to fix what paralegals may have done that was neither correct nor proper. Foreign nationals must have experience lawyers admitted to practice law.

The Law Offices of Brian D. Lerner, APC, handles cases arising from business visas, work permits, Green Cards, non-immigrant visas, deportation, citizenship, appeals and all areas of immigration. The Law Offices of Brian D. Lerner, APC does EB-5 Investor Visas, H-1B Specialty Occupation, L-1 Intracompany Transferee, E-2 Treaty Investor, E-1 Treaty Trader, O-1 Extraordinary Ability among others. Regarding immigrant visas for the Green Card, the firm does PERM and advanced degree PERM, Family Petitions, and Extraordinary Alien Petitions. In addition to affirmative petitions, the Law Firm represents people in deportation and removal hearings, including political asylum, withholding of removal, and convention against torture cases.

Brian D. Lerner has been certified as an expert in Immigration & Nationality Law by the California State Bar, Board of Legal Specialization sicne 2000 and has been re-certified three times. He now passes on his decades of experience by allowing the Reader, Law Schools, Professors and other Immigration Attorneys to purchase sample petitions on every facet of Immigration Law.

TABLE OF CONTENTS

ABOUT THE F-1 APPLICATION

Need a Student Visa? Bogged down by the regulations and requirements? Already been denied? The F-1 Student Visa is just what you need. If approved, then you could come to the U.S. on an F-1 Student Visa and study for years. It will be rejected if not done properly because the officer either does not believe you will return to your home country when you are finished with your F-1 or that you will really not go and get your education.

This sample F-1 Student Visa Petition is for you. It has everything necessary to give you the best chance possible to get an approval. Just input your own information and use the application as a guide. It has been prepared by an expert immigration attorney. Thus, this book will allow you to see a guide of how it is done, prepared and submitted.

SECTION 1
Attorney Cover Letter

LAW OFFICES OF

BRIAN D. LERNER

A PROFESSIONAL CORPORATION

January 27, 2015

USCIS
P.O. Box 660166
Dallas, TX 75266

RE: Reinstatement F-1 Status
Applicant: [redacted]
DOB: 01/09/1978

Dear Sir or Madam:

Ms. [redacted] (hereinafter "Applicant") has been retained our office to file an application to Reinstatement her F-1 visa status.

Hereby we submit the following forms and documents in support of her application:

Form:	**Description:**
G-1145	e-Notification of Application/Petition Acceptance;
G-28	Notice of Entry of Appearance as Attorney;
I-539	Application for Change of Status with $ 290 Filing Fee.

Table of Exhibits:

Exhibit:	**Description:**
1	Declaration of the Applicant;
2	Copy of the Applicant's Expired Passport with Visa and Stamps;
3	Copy of the Applicant's Renewed Passport;
4	The Applicant's Original -94;
5	Copy of the Applicant's I-20;
6	Copy of the Applicant's Transcript; and
7	Copy of the Applicant's Bank Statement.

I.
INTRODUCTION

The Applicant was born on January 9, 1978 in South Africa and she is a citizen of South Africa. **Exhibit 2.** She came to the United State on or around May 17, 2004 with a J-1 visa and worked as an au pair. **Exhibit 2.** Katie Bouvier (hereinafter "Katie") was the Applicant's sponsor. When the au pair program was over the Applicant changed her status from J-1 to F-1 and Katie stayed her sponsor. **Exhibit 3.** She started studying at Moorpark College at 7075 Campus Road, Moorpark, CA 93021. **Exhibit 5.** She was in the pre-nursing program in this school from 2006 to 2011 and received an A.A. degree in Natural Science in December 2011. The Applicant started the Optional Training Program (hereinafter "OPT") on January 1, 2012. During her OPT she was working as a caregiver. Two companies, the 24 Hour Home Care and the Assisted Living, placed her with different clients. **Exhibit 1.**

After the Applicant's OPT was over on January 1, 2013, she transferred to the East Los Angeles College because she wanted to continue her studies and become a nurse. The Applicant finished the full spring semester of 2013 and now wants to continue her studies there. While the Applicant was studying at the East Los Angeles College, she kept working for the same companies as she work during her OPT. She did so because the International Student Services' (hereinafter "ISS") adviser at the Moorpark College told her that she could do that as she transferred to the East Los Angeles College and continued her studies. The Applicant was unaware that she violated her F-1 status. **Exhibit 1.**

II.
THE APPLICANT IS ELIGIBLE FOR REINSTATEMENT HER F-1 STATUS

Under Section 214.2(f)(16) of the 8 C.F.R., an F-1 student is eligible for reinstatement if the student:

- Has not been out of status for more than 5 months at the time of filing the request for reinstatement;
- Does not have a record of repeated or willful violation of [USCIS] regulations;
- Is currently pursuing, or intending to pursue a full course of study in the immediate future at the school which issued the Form I-20;
- Has not engaged in unauthorized employment;
- Is not deportable on any ground other than overstaying or failing to maintain status.

The Applicant fulfills all the requirements but the first one as she has been out of status for more than 5 months at the time of filing the request for reinstatement. However, exceptional circumstances prevented her from filing the request within 5 months. The Applicant did not even know for a long time that she was out of status as she received wrong advise from her ISS. The Applicant did what she supposed to do and asked for advice regarding her employment after her OPT expired from the ISS in the Monroe

College. She was told that it would not be a problem to continue working after the OPT because she transferred to another college and continued her studies. **Exhibit 1.**

Now the Applicant is intending to continue her studies as a full-time student at the East Los Angeles College and become a nurse. **Exhibit 1.**

The Applicant always obeyed to the immigration law of the United States. She does not have a record of repeated and willful immigration violation besides being out of status that was out of her control.

III.
THE VIOLATION OF STATUS RESULTED FROM CIRCUMSTANCES BEYOND THE APPLIANT'S CONTROL.

The Applicant has to establish that the violation of status resulted from circumstances beyond her control. Such circumstances might include serious injury or illness, a natural disaster, or inadvertence, oversight, or neglect on the part of his or her International Student Services adviser.

The Applicant received an A.A. degree in Natural Science in December 2011. After that she was working under her OPT. During her OPT she was working as a caregiver and two companies, the 24 Hour Home Care and the Assisted Living, placed her with different clients. When her OPT expired on January 1, 2013 the Applicant transferred to East Los Angeles College because she wanted to continue her studies and become a nurse. She finished the spring semester of 2013 and wants to continue her studies there. Meanwhile she kept working for the same companies. **Exhibit 1.**

The Applicant continued to work after her OPT ended because she received the advice from the ISS of the Moorpark College that it was all right as she would transfer to the East Los Angeles College and continue her studies. The lady at International Student Service's Office told her that everything would be fine after she transferred to the other college.

The ISS handles student visa issues for foreign students on F-1 visa and the Applicant completely trusted them. She thought the clerks there were familiar with the rules of the student visa. The Applicant did not have the slightest idea that it was not right work after her OPT expired.

Additionally, the Applicant kept working for the same company for a while and she thought that it was just like as a continuance of her OPT. **Exhibit 1.**

Please also note that although her sponsor stopped supporting her financially after she finished her A.A. degree, Katie left her some money that she could live from. This fact shows that the Applicant has enough funding to cover the tuition, fees, and living expenses for the next academic year at the East Los Angeles College. **Exhibit 7.**

Thus, it was out of the Applicant's control that she lost her F-1 status.

IV.

CONCLUSION

For the foregoing reasons, the Applicant prays that her request for Reinstatement her F-1 status be given a favorable consideration.

If you should have any questions, please feel free to contact our office at (562) 495-0554.

Sincerely,

Brian D. Lerner
Attorney at Law

BL:EF: 4191

SECTION 2:
Exhibits

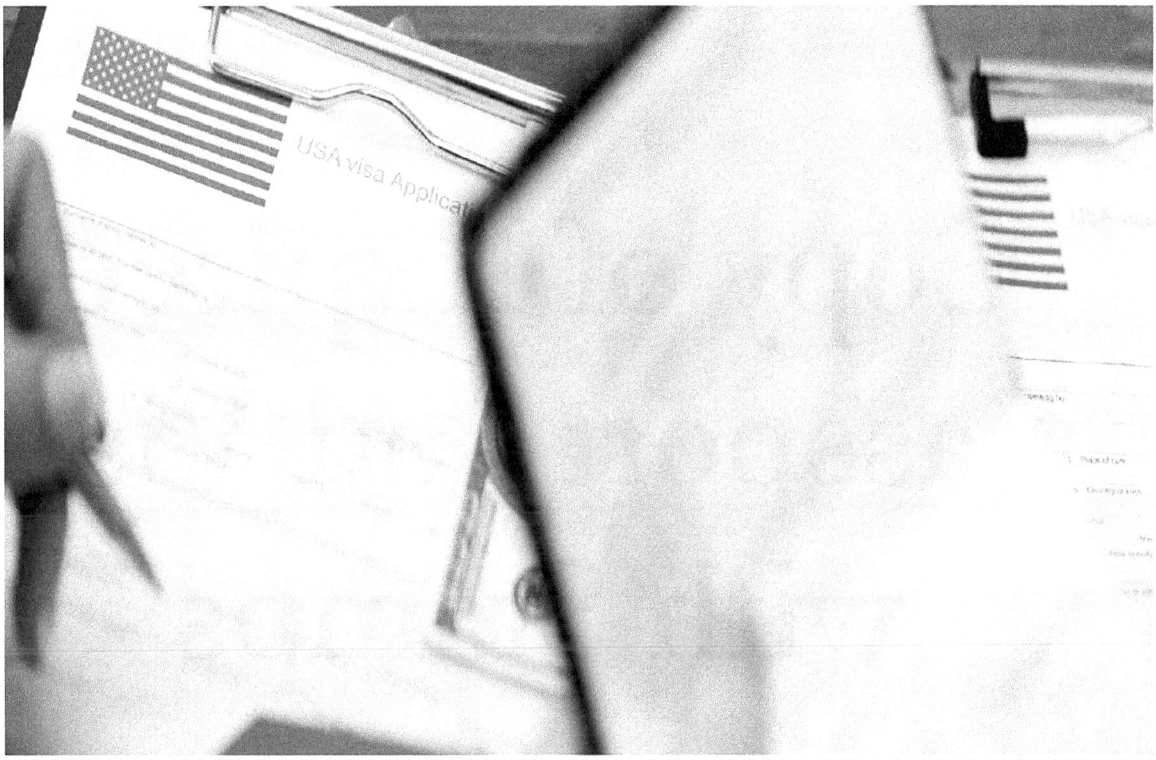

Copy of Expired Passport and Visa with Stamps

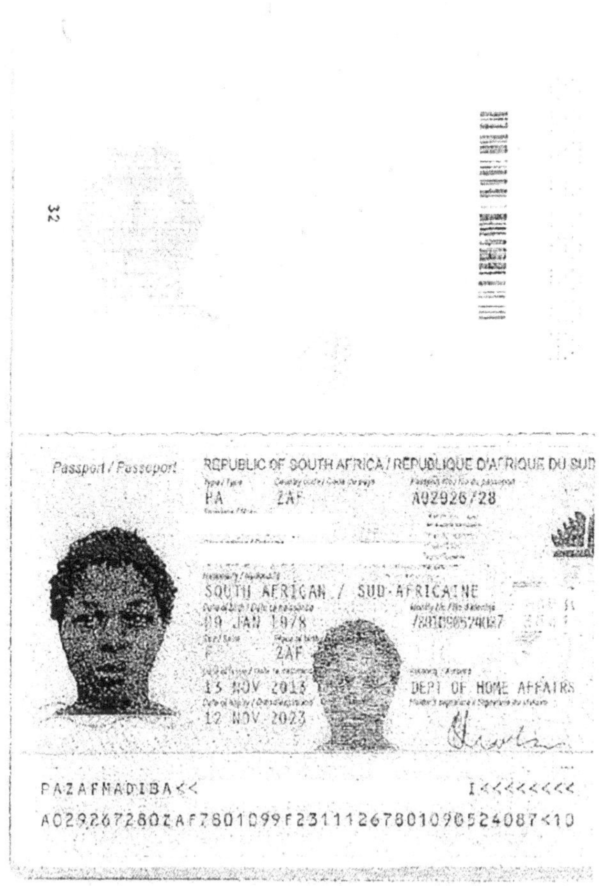

32

Passport / Passeport

REPUBLIC OF SOUTH AFRICA / RÉPUBLIQUE D'AFRIQUE DU SUD

PA ZAF A02926/28

SOUTH AFRICAN / SUD-AFRICAINE

09 JAN 1978

F ZAF

13 NOV 2013

DEPT OF HOME AFFAIRS

12 NOV 2023

PAZAFMADIBA<< I<<<<<<<<

A029267280ZAF7801099F2311126780109052408 7<10

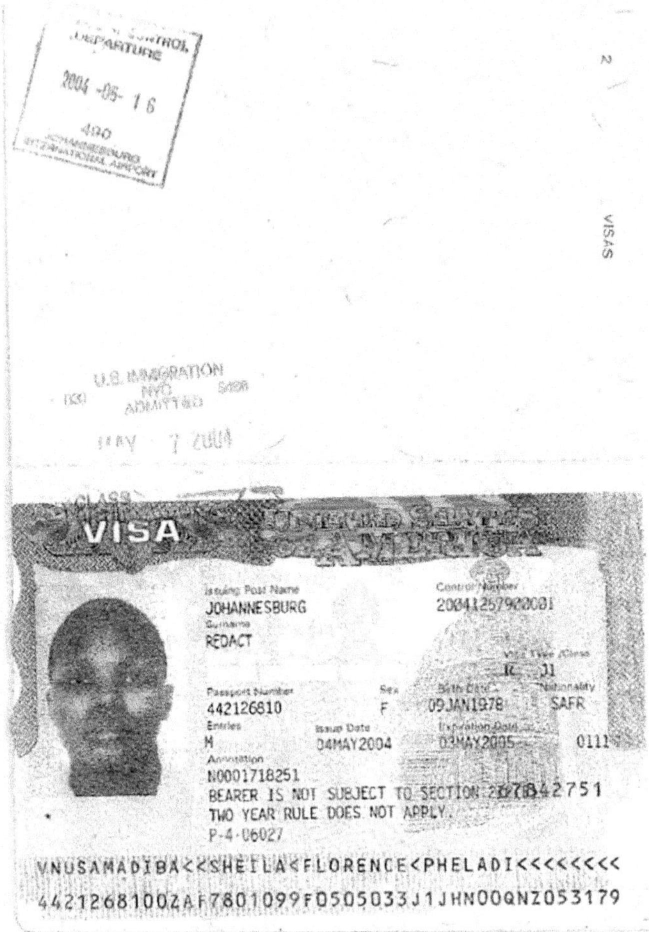
DEPARTURE
2004 -05- 16
490
JOHANNESBURG INTERNATIONAL AIRPORT
VISAS
U.S. IMMIGRATION
NYC
ADMITTED
MAY 7 2004
VISA
Issuing Post Name
JOHANNESBURG
Control Number
20041257920001
Surname
REDACT
Passport Number
442126810
Sex
F
Birth Date
09JAN1978
Nationality
SAFR
Entries
M
Issue Date
04MAY2004
Expiration Date
03MAY2005
0111
Annotation
N0001718251
BEARER IS NOT SUBJECT TO SECTION 212(E)
TWO YEAR RULE DOES NOT APPLY.
P-4-06027
78842751
VNUSAMADIBA<<SHEILA<FLORENCE<PHELADI<<<<<<<<
4421268100ZAF7801099F0505033J1JHN00QNZ053179

Copy of Renewed Passport

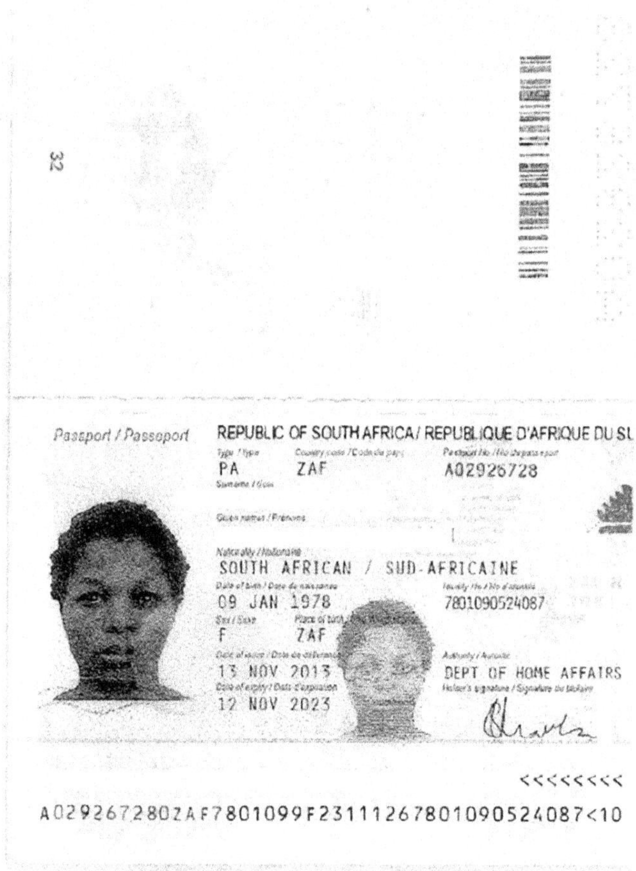

32

Passport / Passeport

REPUBLIC OF SOUTH AFRICA / REPUBLIQUE D'AFRIQUE DU SU

Type / Type: PA

Country code / Code du pays: ZAF

Passport No. / No du passeport: A02926728

Surname / Nom:

Given names / Prénoms:

Nationality / Nationalité: SOUTH AFRICAN / SUD-AFRICAINE

Date of birth / Date de naissance: 09 JAN 1978

Identity No / No d'identité: 7801090524087

Sex / Sexe: F

Place of birth: ZAF

Date of issue / Date de délivrance: 13 NOV 2013

Authority / Autorité: DEPT OF HOME AFFAIRS

Date of expiry / Date d'expiration: 12 NOV 2023

Holder's signature / Signature du titulaire

<<<<<<<<

A0292672807ZAF7801099F2311126780109052408 7<10

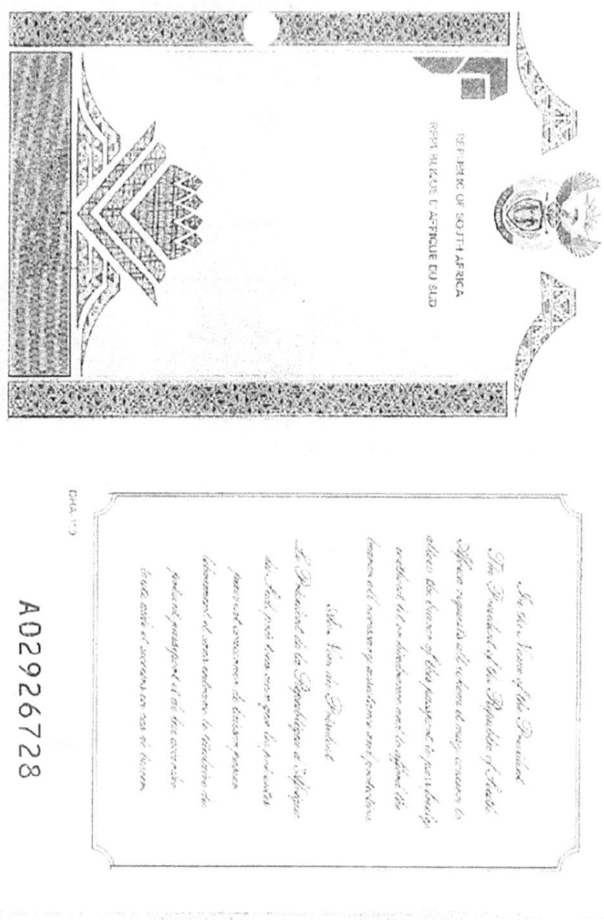
REPUBLIC OF SOUTH AFRICA
RÉPUBLIQUE D'AFRIQUE DU SUD
A02926728

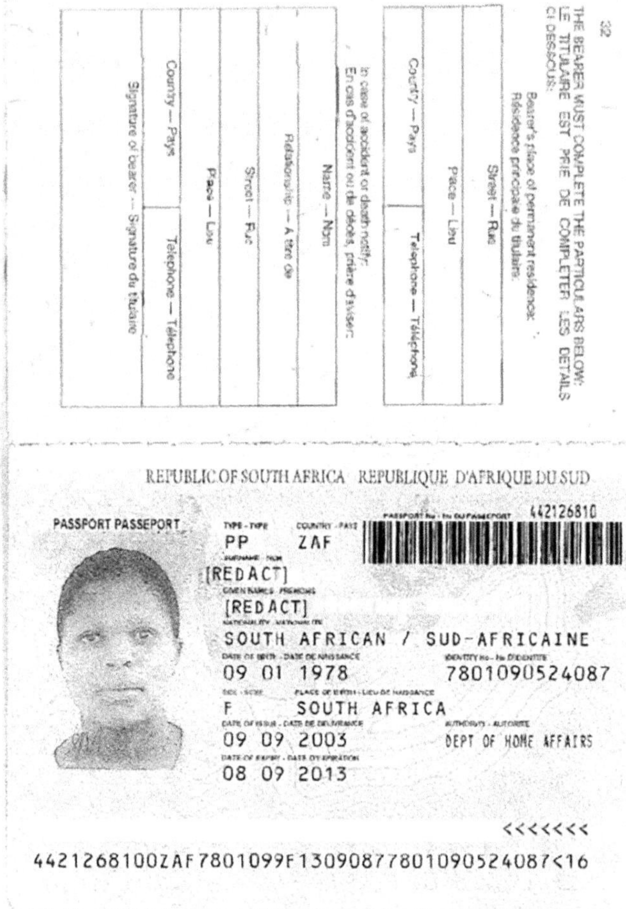

32

THE BEARER MUST COMPLETE THE PARTICULARS BELOW:
LE TITULAIRE EST PRIE DE COMPLETER LES DETAILS CI DESSOUS:

Bearer's place of permanent residence:
Résidence principale du titulaire:

Street — Rue

Place — Lieu

Country — Pays | Telephone — Téléphone

In case of accident or death notify:
En cas d'accident ou de décès, prière d'aviser:

Name — Nom

Relationship — A titre de

Street — Rue

Place — Lieu

Country — Pays | Telephone — Téléphone

Signature of bearer — Signature du titulaire

REPUBLIC OF SOUTH AFRICA REPUBLIQUE D'AFRIQUE DU SUD

PASSPORT PASSEPORT

TYPE - TYPE: PP
COUNTRY - PAYS: ZAF
PASSPORT No - No DU PASSEPORT: 442126810

SURNAME - NOM: [REDACT]

GIVEN NAMES - PRENOMS: [REDACT]

NATIONALITY - NATIONALITE: SOUTH AFRICAN / SUD-AFRICAINE

DATE OF BIRTH - DATE DE NAISSANCE: 09 01 1978
IDENTITY No - No D'IDENTITE: 7801090524087

SEX - SEXE: F
PLACE OF BIRTH - LIEU DE NAISSANCE: SOUTH AFRICA

DATE OF ISSUE - DATE DE DELIVRANCE: 09 09 2003
AUTHORITY - AUTORITE: DEPT OF HOME AFFAIRS

DATE OF EXPIRY - DATE D'EXPIRATION: 08 09 2013

<<<<<<<

4421268100ZAF7801099F1309087801090524087<16

Applicant's Original I-94

case 4191

Departure Number

090403684 11

U.S. IMMIGRATION NYC 6468 ADMITTED

Immigration and Naturalization Service

MAY 17 2004

I-94
Departure Record

J1

CLASS D/S
UNTIL

14. Family Name MADIBA

15. First (Given) Name SHEILA

16. Birth Date (Day/Mo/Yr) 09/01/78

17. Country of Citizenship South Africa

See Other Side

STAPLE HERE

Warning - A nonimmigrant who accepts unauthorized employment is subject to deportation.

Important - Retain this permit in your possession; *you must surrender it when you leave the U.S.* Failure to do so may delay your entry into the U.S. in the future. You are authorized to stay in the U.S. only until the date written on this form. To remain past this date, without permission from immigration authorities, is a violation of the law.

Surrender this permit when you leave the U.S.:

- By sea or air, to the transportation line.
- Across the Canadian border, to a Canadian Official.
- Across the Mexican border, to a U.S. Official.

Students planning to reenter the U.S. within 30 days to return to the same school, see "Arrival-Departure" on page 2 of Form I-20 prior to surrendering this permit.

Record of Changes

AuPair

N0001718251 P-4-06027

AuPair Care Inc

Port:

Departure Record

Date:

Carrier:

Flight #/Ship Name:

Copy of Applicant’s I-20

U.S. Department of Justice
Immigration and Naturalization Service

Certificate of Eligibility for Nonimmigrant (F-1) Student Status - For Academic and Language Students (OMB NO. 1653-[illegible]8) Page 1

Please read Instructions on Page 2
This page must be completed and signed in the U.S. by a designated school official.

SEVIS Student's Code: N0003117[illegible]

1. Family Name (surname): Nadiba
First (given) name: Sheila
Middle Name: V.
Country of birth: SOUTH AFRICA
Date of birth (mo/day/year): 01/09/1978
Country of citizenship: SOUTH AFRICA
Admission number:

For Immigration Official Use

Visa issuing post | Date Visa Issued

Reinstated, extension granted to:

2. School (School district) name:
Moorpark College
Ventura County Community College Distric
School Official to be notified of student's arrival in U.S. (Name and Title):
Maureen Rauchfuss
Matriculation Spec II, Admissions, PDSO
School address (include zip code):
7075 Campus Rd.
Moorpark, CA 93021
School code (including 3-digit suffix, if any) and approval date:
LOS214F20325000 approved on 02/07/2003

3. This certificate is issued to the student named above for:
Continued attendance at this school.

4. Level of education the student is pursuing or will pursue in the United States:
ASSOCIATE

5. The student named above has been accepted for a full course of study at this school, majoring in Natural Sciences
The student is expected to report to the school no later than 08/17/2009 and complete studies not later than 12/21/2011. The normal length of study is 36 months.

6. English proficiency:
This school requires English proficiency.
The student has the required English proficiency.

7. This school estimates the student's average costs for an academic term of 12 (up to 12) months to be:

a.	Tuition and fees	$ 5,500.00
b.	Living expenses	$ 12,000.00
c.	Expenses of dependents (0)	$ 0.00
d.	Other (specify): Medical Insura	$ 750.00
	Total	$ 18,250.00

8. This school has information showing the following as the student's means of support, estimated for an academic term of 12 months (Use the same number of months given in item 7).

a.	Student's personal funds	$ 0.00
b.	Funds from this school Specify type:	$ 0.00
c.	Funds from another source Specify type: Sponsor: Katherine Bowler	$ 57,287.00
d.	On-campus employment	$ 0.00
	Total	$ 57,287.00

9. Remarks: Student will complete her Associate degree in Natural Sciences on 12/21/11 and will seek employment in that area of study as she plans to go into Nursing later.

10. School Certification: I certify under penalty of perjury that all information provided above in items 1 through 9 was completed before I signed this form and is true and correct; I executed this form in the United States after review and evaluation in the United States by me or other officials of the school of the student's application, transcripts, or other records of courses taken and proof of financial responsibility, which were received at the school prior to the execution of this form; the school has determined that the above named student's qualifications meet all standards for admission to the school; the student will be required to pursue a full course of study as defined by 8 CFR 214.2(f)(6). I am a designated official of the above named school and am authorized to issue this form.

Maureen Rauchfuss	[signature]	Matriculation Spec II, Admissions, PDSO	11/04/2011	Moorpark, CA
Name of School Official	Signature of Designated School Official	Title	Date Issued	Place Issued (city and state)

11. Student Certification: I have read and agreed to comply with the terms and conditions of my admission and those of any extension of stay as specified on page 2. I certify that all information provided on this form refers specifically to me and is true and correct to the best of my knowledge. I certify that I seek to enter or remain in the United States temporarily, and solely for the purpose of pursuing a full course of study at the school named on page 1 of this form. I also authorize the named school to release any information from my records which is needed by the INS pursuant to 8 CFR 214.3(g) to determine my nonimmigrant status.

Sheila Nadiba	[signature]	[illegible]
Name of Student	Signature of Student	Date

Name of parent or guardian if student under 18	Signature of parent or guardian	Address (city)	(State or Province) (Country)	(Date)

Form I-20 A-B (Rev. 04-27-88)N

For Official Use Only

Authority for collecting the information on this and related student forms is contained in 8 U.S.C. 1101 and 1184. The information solicited will be used by the Department of State and the Immigration and Naturalization Service to determine eligibility for the benefits requested.

INSTRUCTIONS TO DESIGNATED SCHOOL OFFICIALS

1. **The law provides severe penalties for knowingly and willfully falsifying or concealing a material fact or using any false document in the submission of this form.** Designated school officials should consult regulations pertaining to the issuance of Form I-20 A-B at 8 CFR 214.3(k) before completing this form. Failure to comply with these regulations may result in the withdrawal of the school approval for attendance by foreign students by the Immigration and Naturalization Service (8 CFR 214.4).

2. ISSUANCE OF FORM I-20 A-B. Designated school officials may issue a Form I-20 A-B to a student who fits into one of the following categories, if the student has been accepted for full-time attendance at the institution: a) a prospective F-1 nonimmigrant student; b) an F-1 transfer student; c) an F-1 student advancing to a higher educational level at the same institution; d) an out of status student seeking reinstatement. The form may also be issued to the dependent spouse or child of an F-1 student for securing entry into the United States.

When issuing a Form I-20 A-B, designated school officials should complete the student's admission number whenever possible to ensure proper data entry and record keeping.

3. ENDORSEMENT OF PAGE 3 FOR REENTRY. Designated school officials may endorse page 3 of the Form I-20 A-B for reentry if the student and/or the F-2 dependents is to leave the United States temporarily. This should be done only when the information on the Form I-20 remains unchanged. If there have been substantial changes in item 4, 5, 7, or 8, a new Form I-20 A-B should be issued.

4. REPORTING REQUIREMENT. Designated school officials should always forward the top page of the form I-20 A-B to the INS data processing center at P.O. Box 140, London, Kentucky 40741 for data entry except when the form is issued to an F-1 student for initial entry or reentry into the United States, or for reinstatement to student status. (Requests for reinstatement should be sent to the Immigration and Naturalization Service district office having jurisdiction over the student's temporary residence in this country.)

The INS data processing center will return this top page to the issuing school for disposal after data entry and microfilming.

5. CERTIFICATION. Designated school officials should certify on the bottom part of page 1 of this form that the Form I-20 A-B is completed and issued in accordance with the pertinent regulations. The designated school official should remove the carbon sheet from the completed and signed Form I-20 A-B before forwarding it to the student.

6. ADMISSION RECORDS. Since the Immigration and Naturalization Service may request information concerning the student's immigration status for various reasons, designated school officials should retain all evidence which shows the scholastic ability and financial status on which admission was based, until the school has reported the student's termination of studies to the Immigration and Naturalization Service.

INSTRUCTIONS TO STUDENTS

1. **Student Certification.** You should read everything on this page carefully and be sure that you understand the terms and conditions concerning your admission and stay in the United States as a nonimmigrant student before you sign the student certification on the bottom part of page 1. **The law provides severe penalties for knowingly and willfully falsifying or concealing a material fact, or using any false document in the submission of this form.**

2. ADMISSION. A nonimmigrant student may be admitted for duration of status. This means that you are authorized to stay in the United States for the entire length of time during which you are enrolled as a full-time student in an educational program and any period of authorized practical training plus sixty days. While in the United States, you must maintain a valid foreign passport unless you are exempt from passport requirements.

You may continue from one educational level to another, such as progressing from high school to a bachelor's program or a bachelor's program to a master's program, etc., simply by invoking the procedures for school transfers.

Form I-20 A-B (Rev. 04-27-88)N

3. SCHOOL. For initial admission, you must attend the school specified on your visa. If you have a Form I-20 A-B from more than one school, it is important to have the name of the school you intend to attend specified on your visa by presenting a Form I-20 A-B from that school to the visa issuing consular officer. Failure to attend the specified school will result in the loss of your student status and subject you to deportation.

4. REENTRY. A nonimmigrant student may be readmitted after a temporary absence of five months or less from the United States, if the student is otherwise admissible. You may be readmitted by presenting a valid foreign passport, a valid visa, and either a new Form I-20 A-B or a page 3 of the Form I-20 A-B (the ID Copy) properly endorsed for reentry if the information on the I-20 form is current.

5. TRANSFER. A nonimmigrant student is permitted to transfer to a different school provided the transfer procedure is followed. To transfer schools, you should first notify the school you are attending of the intent to transfer, then obtain a Form I-20 A-B from the school you intend to attend. Transfer will be effected only if you return the Form I-20 A-B to the designated school official within 15 days of beginning attendance at the new school. The designated school official will then report the transfer to the Immigration and Naturalization Service.

6. EXTENSION OF STAY. If you cannot complete the educational program after having been in student status for longer than the anticipated length of the program plus a grace period in a single educational level, or for more than eight consecutive years, you must apply for extension of stay. An application for extension of stay on a Form I-538 should be filed with the Immigration and Naturalization Service district office having jurisdiction over your school at least 15 days but no more than 60 days before the expiration of your authorized stay.

7. EMPLOYMENT. As an F-1 student, you are not permitted to work off-campus or to engage in business without specific employment authorization. After your first year in F-1 student status, you may apply for employment authorization on Form I-538 based on financial needs arising after receiving student status, or the need to obtain practical training.

8. **Notice of Address.** If you move, you must submit a notice within 10 days of the change of address to the Immigration and Naturalization Service. (Form AR-11 is available at any INS office.)

9. **Arrival/Departure.** When you leave the United States, you must surrender your Form I-94 Departure Record. Please see back side of Form I-94 for detailed instructions. You do not have to turn in the I-94 if you are visiting Canada, Mexico, or adjacent islands other than Cuba for less than 30 days.

10. **Financial Support.** You must demonstrate that you are financially able to support yourself for the entire period of stay in the United States while pursuing a full course of study. You are required to attach documentary evidence of means of support.

11. **Authorization to Release Information by School.** To comply with requests from the United States Immigration & Naturalization Service for information concerning your immigration status, you are required to give authorization to the named school to release such information from your records. The school will provide the Service your name, country of birth, current address, and any other information on a regular basis or upon request.

12. **Penalty.** To maintain your nonimmigrant student status, you must be enrolled as a full-time student at the school you are authorized to attend. You may engage in employment only when you have received permission to work. Failure to comply with these regulations will result in the loss of your student status and subject you to deportation.

AUTHORITY FOR COLLECTING. Authority for collecting the information on this and related student forms is contained in 8 U.S.C. 1101 and 1184. The information solicited will be used by the Department of State and the Immigration and Naturalization Service to determine eligibility for the benefits requested. The law provides severe penalties for knowingly and willfully falsifying or concealing a material fact, or using any false document in the submission of this form.

REPORTING BURDEN. Public reporting burden for this collection of information is estimated to average 30 minutes per response, including the time for reviewing instructions, searching existing data sources, gathering and maintaining the data needed, and completing and reviewing the collection of information. Send comments regarding this burden estimate or any other aspect of this collection of information, including suggestions for reducing this burden, to: U.S. Department of Justice, Immigration and Naturalization Service (Room 2011), Washington, D.C. 20536, and to the Office of Management and Budget, Paperwork Reduction Project, OMB No. 1653-0038, Washington, D.C. 20503.

IF YOU NEED MORE INFORMATION CONCERNING YOUR F-1 NONIMMIGRANT STUDENT STATUS AND THE RELATING IMMIGRATION PROCEDURES, PLEASE CONTACT EITHER YOUR FOREIGN STUDENT ADVISOR ON CAMPUS OR A NEARBY IMMIGRATION AND NATURALIZATION SERVICE OFFICE.

SEVIS

Student #

N000311[illegible]7

FAMILY NAME: ______ FIRST NAME: ______

Primary Major: 30.1801 Natural Sciences

Student Employment Authorization:

Employment Status: FULL TIME Type: OPT

Duration of Employment - From (Date): 01/02/2012 To (Date): 01/01/2013

Employer Name:

Employer Location:

The Student has met the 1 full academic year requirement.

Comments: If OPT is issued later than 1/2/2012 then please extend end date to give student the full year of employment.

Event History

Event Name:	Event Date:
Registration	05/16/2010

Current Authorizations:	Start Date:	End Date:
OPT Employment Requested	01/02/2012	01/01/2013

This page when properly endorsed, may be used for reentry of the student to attend the same school after a temporary absence from the United States. Each certification signature is valid for one year.

Name of School:

Name of School Official	Signature of Designated School Official	Title	Date Issued	Place Issued (city and state)
Maureen Rauchfuss		Matriculation Spec II, - Admissions, PDSO	11/04/2011	Moorpark, CA
Name of School Official	Signature of Designated School Official	Title	Date Issued	Place Issued (city and state)
Name of School Official	Signature of Designated School Official	Title	Date Issued	Place Issued (city and state)
Name of School Official	Signature of Designated School Official	Title	Date Issued	Place Issued (city and state)

REDACTED

Receipt Number WAC-06-158-50362

Immigration and

Naturalization Service

I-94

Departure Record Petitioner:

14. Family Name
REDACTED

15. First (Given) Name
REDACTED

16. Date of Birth
01/09/1978

17. Country of Citizenship
SOUTH AFRICA

Activity summary

Beginning balance on 09/06	$8,850.97
Deposits/Additions	26,751.14
Withdrawals/Subtractions	-8,132.9
Ending balance on 10/07	$27,479.21

Account number: REDACTED
REDACTED
California account terms and conditions apply
For Direct Deposit and Automatic Payments use Routing Number (RTN): 121042882

Overdraft Protection

This account is not currently covered by Overdraft Protection. If you would like more information regarding Overdraft Protection and eligibility requirements please call the number listed at the top of your statement or visit your Wells Fargo branch.

Wells Fargo Exclusive Rewards

Total points available as of 10/06/2013	7 806
Points earned in the month of September	27
Points redeemed in the month of December	0

Get your most current point balance and redeem rewards at WellsFargoRewards.com or call 1-888-245-1584

Transaction history

Date	Check Number	Description	Deposits/ Additions	Withdrawals/ Subtractions	Ending daily balance
09/7		Check Crd Purchase 09/07 Alf Pharmacy, Valley Sherman Oaks CA 486027xxxxx3202 254140019217154 ?McC=5912 01		38.41	
09/8		Check Crd Purchase 09/08 Exxonmobil 11515624 Los Angeles 486827xxxxx3202 254149015700341 ?McC=5542		567.61	8,254.9
09/11		Online Transfer From Douglas H Ref #lbeo2K32K8 Checking Supply Parts December	13,375.57		21,630.:
09/24		Check Crd Purchase 09/24 Van Nuys Zankou Inc Van Nuys CA 486827xxxxx3202 268140014978815 ?McC=5812 90		560.00	21,070.5
10/2		Online Transfer From Douglas H Ref #lbeufybxtk Checking Supply Parts October	13,375.57		
10/3		POS Purchase - 10/03 Mach ID 000000 Arco Paypoint Van Nuys CA 3202 0058127881446805 ?McC=5542		605.00	33,641.0
10/3		Check Crd Purchase 10/03 7-Eleven 17888 San Fernando CA 486827xxxxx3202 275140009682976 ?McC=5541		19.27	33,021.8
10/4		Check Crd Purchase 10/04 Alf Pharmacy, Valley Sherman Oaks CA 486827xxxxx3202 280140008884139 ?McC=5912		2,000.00	31,621.8
10/4		Check Crd Purchase 10/04 Carl's Jr 1103404 Los Angeles CA 486827xxxxx3202 263140008226780 ?McC=5814		2,587.78	
10/5		POS Purchase - 10/06 Mach ID 000000 Cvs 04782 04782 Van Nuys CA 3202 003012839183877460 ?McC=		1,594.85	
Ending balance on 10/7				10.00	27,471.21
Totals			$26,751.14	8,132.9	

The Ending Daily Balance does not reflect any pending withdrawals or holds on deposited funds that may have been outstanding on your account when your transactions posted. If you had insufficient available funds when a transaction posted, fees may have been assessed.

Your Checking Package is designed to work with you to achieve financial success by providing additional benefits on the accounts and services you need. Remember, to waive the monthly service fee on your checking account, you must meet the Checking Package requirements and have three additional qualifying accounts and/or services. If you have any questions, please contact your Wells Fargo banker or call Wells Fargo Phone Bank at 1-800-TO-WELLS (1-800-869-3557).

IMPORTANT ACCOUNT INFORMATION

We want to keep you informed of upcoming changes to your Custom Management Checking account. Effective November 14, 2012, the options to waive your monthly service fee with a complete package will change to the following:
- A qualifying direct deposit of $500 or more, OR
- $1,500 minimum daily balance, OR
- A monthly automatic loan payment from this account to a Wells Fargo home equity/personal loan or line of credit, or Wells Fargo Home Mortgage loan

Otherwise $10 (If you have online statements for this account you will receive a $2 discount on the monthly service fee)
Please review the new criteria carefully, as the automatic transfer waiver option is no longer available and it may be necessary for you to take action to meet the new requirements in order to waive the monthly service fee. For questions, please contact your local banker or call the phone number listed at the top of your statement.

Enjoy safe and secure savings with a Wells Fargo Time Account (CD). You will get a guaranteed rate of return and have the peace of mind of knowing your money is FDIC insured up to applicable limits. Talk with your Wells Fargo Banker today.

Turn off the paper clutter . . . If you bank online, get your statement online. It's easy to switch to Online Only Statements. Sign on at wellsfargo.com/turnoffpaper, select Online Only, or check the box Switch All to Online Only Delivery and click Submit at the bottom of the page. Online statements reduce paper clutter, help protect against identity theft, and they're gentle on the environment.

Worksheet to balance your account

Follow the steps below to reconcile your statement balance with your account register balance. Be sure that your register shows any interest paid into your account and any service charges, automatic payments or ATM transactions withdrawn from your account during this statement period.

[A] **Enter the ending balance on this statement.** $ ______

[B] **List outstanding deposits and other credits to your account that do not appear on this statement.** Enter the total in the column to the right.

Description	Amount
Total	$

+ $ ______

[C] **Add [A] and [B] to calculate the subtotal.** = $ ______

[D] **List outstanding checks, withdrawals, and other debits to your account that do not appear on the statement.** Enter the total in the column to the right.

Number/Description	Amount
Total	$

- $ ______

[E] **Subtract [D] from [C] to calculate the adjusted ending balance.** This amount should be the same as the current balance shown in your register. = $ ______

General statement policies for Wells Fargo Bank

- **To dispute or report inaccuracies in information we have furnished to a Consumer Reporting Agency about your accounts.** You have the right to dispute the accuracy of information that Wells Fargo Bank, N.A. has furnished to a consumer reporting agency by writing to us at Wells Fargo Servicing, P.O. Box 14415, Des Moines, IA 50306-3415. Please describe the specific information that is inaccurate or in dispute and the basis for the dispute along with supporting documentation. If you believe the information furnished is the result of identity theft, please provide us with an identity theft report.

- **In case of errors or questions about your electronic transfers,** telephone us at the number printed on the front of this statement or write us at Wells Fargo Bank, P.O. Box 6995, Portland, OR 97228-6995 as soon as you can, if you think your statement or receipt is wrong or if you need more information about a transfer on the statement or receipt. We must hear from you no later than 60 days after we sent you the FIRST statement on which the error or problem appeared.

  1. Tell us your name and account number (if any).
  2. Describe the error or the transfer you are unsure about, and explain as clearly as you can why you believe it is an error or why you need more information.
  3. Tell us the dollar amount of the suspected error.

  We will investigate your complaint and will correct any error promptly. If we take more than 10 business days to do this, we will credit your account for the amount you think is in error, so that you will have the use of the money during the time it takes us to complete our investigation.

- **In case of errors or questions about your Direct Deposit Advance service**

  If you think your bill is wrong, or if you need more information about a transaction on your bill, write us at Wells Fargo Bank, P. O. Box 6995, Portland, OR 97228-6995 as soon as possible. We must hear from you no later than 60 days after we sent you the first bill on which the error or problem appeared. You can telephone us but doing so will not preserve your rights.

  In your letter, give us the following information.

  1. Your name and account number
  2. The dollar amount of the suspected error
  3. Describe the error and explain, if you can, why you believe there is an error. If you need more information, describe the item you are unsure about.

  You do not have to pay any amount in question while we are investigating but you are still obligated to pay the parts of your bill that are not in question. While we investigate your question, we cannot report you as delinquent or take any action to collect the amount you question.

Applicant's Transcript (Sealed)

LOS ANGELES MISSION COLLEGE
ITV - The Weekend College
13356 Eldridge Ave.
Sylmar, CA 91342-3244

LAMC

Hasler

US POS

OFFICIAL TRANSCRIPT ENCLOSED

ADDRESS TO:
REDACTED
BOX 570822
TARZANA CA REC

To be valid, this POSTALBOXX™ field must display

91357$0822 B007

EAST LOS ANGELES COLLEGE
Admissions Office / Transcript Unit
1301 Avenida Cesar Chavez
Monterey Park, CA 91754

SANTA ANA
CA 926
20 NOV '14
PM 1 L
FIRST CLASS

OFFICIAL TRANSCRIPT ENCLOSE

ADDRESS TO:

1712 SINALOA RD, APT 202
SIMI VALLEY CA 93065

93065306552

Applicant's Bank Statement

Wells Fargo StoreVision Platform

Search | Sales | Banker Toolbox | Administration | Main | Sign Off   Quick Profile | Clear List   Customer List (0) |

Account

Wells Fargo Goal Savings

Bank CALIFORNIA (114) Detail | Address | History | Statements | Stop Payments | Holds/Pledges | Overdraft/NSF Fees | Service Fees | Check Orders | Transfers | Customer Event History | Documents

Checking/Savings Account History

Select action ...

Tax Responsible Customer	REDACTED Sole Owner
Additional Customers	None
Ledger Balance	$20,699.09
Available Balance	$20,799.09
Regulation D Withdrawals	0 (Current Service Charge Cycle)

Date	Description	Check Number	Amount	Balance
01/05/15	Atm 4380x 5823 Kanan Agoura Ca Card8307	(pending)	+1610.00	
01/05/15	Atm 9943n 6001 Topang Woodland Hill Ca Card8307	(pending)	100.00	
01/02/15	Atm Withdrawal Authorized On 01/02 Baldwin Hills (alberts Lod Angeles Ca 0003665 Atm Id 5876c Card 8307		40.00	20699.09
12/31/14	Monthly Service Fee Reversal		+5.00	20739.09
12/31/14	Monthly Service Fee		5.00	20734.09
12/31/14	Interest Payment		+0.17	20739.09
12/22/14	Atm Transfer Authorized On 12/20 From Sheila F Pheladi-madiba Checking Westlake Village Offi Westlake Vill Ca 0003461 Atm Id 0737l Card 8307		+1000.00	20738.92
12/08/14	Atm Transfer Authorized On 12/06 To Sheila F Pheladi-madiba Checking 925 Broadbeck Dr. Newbury Ca 0009987 Atm Id 9916c Card 8307		600.00	19738.92
12/05/14	Float Adjustment			20338.92
12/05/14	Atm Check Deposit On 12/05 5823 Kanan Road Agoura Ca 0006392 Atm Id 4380w Card 8307 View Deposit		+1740.00	20338.92
11/28/14	Monthly Service Fee Reversal		+5.00	18598.92
11/28/14	Monthly Service Fee		5.00	18593.92
11/28/14	Interest Payment		+0.14	18598.92
11/28/14	Atm Transfer On From Sheila F Pheladi-madiba Checking 5823 Kanan Road Agoura Ca 8307 0		+1000.00	18598.78
11/21/14	Atm Withdrawal - 5823 Kanan Road Agoura Ca 8307 0003562		20.00	17598.78
11/17/14	Atm Transfer On To Sheila F Pheladi-madiba Checking 5823 Kanan Road Agoura Ca 8307 000		200.00	17618.78
11/10/14	Atm Transfer On From Sheila F Pheladi-madiba Checking 1919 N Campus Ave. Bldg 9 Ca 8307 0		+1000.00	17818.78
11/07/14	Atm Withdrawal - 5823 Kanan Road Agoura Ca 8307 0000524		20.00	16818.78
11/05/14	Tele-transfer To Checking Xxxxxx1028 Reference # Tfek6cgz2g		60.00	16838.78
11/03/14	Atm Transfer On To Sheila F Pheladi-madiba Checking 5823 Kanan Road Agoura Ca 8307 000		20.00	16898.78
11/03/14	Atm Withdrawal - 140 E Thousand Oaks Thousand Oaks Ca		20.00	16918.78

	8307 0007415		
11/03/14	Atm Transfer On To Sheila F Pheladi-madiba Checking Westlake Village Offi Westlake Vill Ca 8307 000	100.00	16938.78
11/03/14	Atm Withdrawal - Westlake Village Offi Westlake Vill Ca 8307 0001055	20.00	17038.78
10/31/14	Monthly Service Fee Reversal	+5.00	17058.78
10/31/14	Monthly Service Fee	5.00	17053.78
10/31/14	Interest Payment	+0.13	17058.78
10/27/14	Atm Transfer On To Sheila F Pheladi-madiba Checking 6001 Topanga Cyn Woodland Hill Ca 8307 000	40.00	17058.65
10/27/14	Atm Withdrawal - 6001 Topanga Cyn Woodland Hill Ca 8307 0005794	40.00	17098.65
10/27/14	Atm Withdrawal - 6001 Topanga Cyn Woodland Hill Ca 8307 0005793	20.00	17138.65
10/24/14	Atm Withdrawal - 5823 Kanan Road Agoura Ca 8307 0007357	20.00	17158.65
10/24/14	Atm Transfer On To Sheila F Pheladi-madiba Checking 5823 Kanan Road Agoura Ca 8307 000	100.00	17178.65
10/24/14	Float Adjustment		17278.65
10/24/14	Atm Check Deposit - 5823 Kanan Road Agoura Ca 8307 0007355 View Deposit	+1610.00	17278.65
10/20/14	Atm Withdrawal - 5823 Kanan Road Agoura Ca 8307 0006692	20.00	15668.65
10/14/14	Atm Transfer On To Sheila F Pheladi-madiba Checking 140 E Thousand Oaks Thousand Oaks Ca 8307 000	200.00	15688.65
10/14/14	Atm Withdrawal - 140 E Thousand Oaks Thousand Oaks Ca 8307 0001658	80.00	15888.65
10/10/14	Atm Withdrawal - 5823 Kanan Road Agoura Ca 8307 0004516	140.00	15968.65
10/10/14	Atm Transfer On To Sheila F Pheladi-madiba Checking 5823 Kanan Road Agoura Ca 8307 000	500.00	16108.65
10/10/14	Float Adjustment		16608.65
10/10/14	Atm Check Deposit - 5823 Kanan Road Agoura Ca 8307 0004514 View Deposit	+1480.00	16608.65
10/06/14	Atm Transfer On To Sheila F Pheladi-madiba Checking 5823 Kanan Road Agoura Ca 8307 000	100.00	15128.65

SECTION 3:
Supporting Applicant's Declaration

DECLARATION OF [NEW APPLICANT]
IN SUPPORT OF APPLICATION FOR REINSTATEMENT OF F-1 VISA

I, ██████ hereby declare as follows:

1. I am giving this declaration in support my application for reinstatement my F-1 Visa in the United States.

2. Currently, I reside at [REDACTED].

3. I was born on January 9, 1978 in [REDACTED].

4. I came to the United State on or around May 17, 2004 with a J-1 visa and worked as an aupair for my sponsor, Katie Bouvier (hereinafter "Katie"). When the aupair program was over I changed my status from J-1 to F-1. Katie stayed my sponsor.

5. I started studying at Moorpark College at 7075 Campus Road, Moorpark, CA 93021. I was in the pre-nursing program in this school from [REDACTED]. I received an A.A. degree in Natural Science in December 2011.

6. I started the Optional Training Program (OPT) on January 1, 2012 that expired on January 1, 2013.

7. I transferred to East Los Angeles College because I wanted to continue my studies and become a nurse. I have not earned a degree there yet just finished the full spring semester of 2013. That is why I would like to continue my studies there.

8. During my OPT I was working as a caregiver. Two companies, the 24 Hour Home Care and the Assisted Living, placed me with different clients. I worked at 24 Hour Home Care in Culver City taking care of two persons who have Muscular Dystrophy.

9. During my studies Katie sponsored me. She was very good and supportive but in 2012 Katie told me that she and her husband had financial difficulties and could not sponsor me any more. Ultimately, they ended up selling their house. She sponsored me until I finished my A.A. degree.

10. Even though Katie could not sponsor me any more, she left me some money that I could live from. Also, I continued to work after the OPT ended because I received the advice from the Designated School Official (DSO) of the Moorpark College that it was all right as I would be fine transfer to the East Los Angeles College. The lady at the office told me that everything will be fine after I would transfer to the other school.

11. The DSO handles student visa issues for foreign students on F-1 visa and I completely trusted them. I thought the clerks there were familiar with the rules of the student visa. Honestly, I had no idea that I could not work after my OPT expired.

12. Additionally, I kept working for the same company for a while and I thought that it counted just a continuance of my OPT.

13. I hope and pray that I will get a chance to stay in the United States and fulfill my dream and become a nurse.

I declare under penalty of perjury pursuant to the laws of the State of California that the forgoing declaration is true and correct to the best of my knowledge. Executed in Simi Valley, California.

DATED: 01 August 2014 DECLARANT: [signature]

www.ingramcontent.com/pod-product-compliance
Lightning Source LLC
LaVergne TN
LVHW060045210926
848481LV00013B/3960